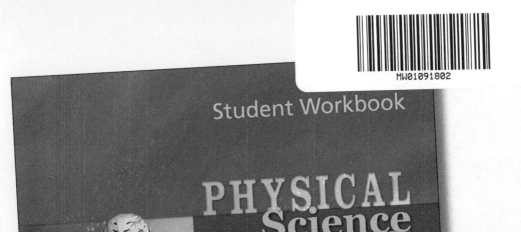

Student Workbook

PHYSICAL
Science
AGS

Key Features:

- One activity per lesson helps you foster integral Physical Science skills
- Master key vocabulary using vocabulary reviews and games
- Develop math proficiency and conceptual understanding with problem-based activities
- Review key concepts with Compare and Contrast activities

PEARSON

ALWAYS LEARNING

by
Robert H. Marshall
Donald H. Jacobs

Glenview, Illinois • Boston, Massachusetts • Chandler, Arizona • Upper Saddle River, New Jersey

ISBN-13: 978-0-785-47071-7
ISBN-10:   0-785-47071-9

PEARSON

ISBN-13: 978-0-78547071-7
ISBN-10:   0-785-47071-9
8 19

Table of Contents

What Is Physical Science?

Directions Read each statement. Then unscramble the letters in parentheses. Each statement is a clue for the term. Write the term on the line.

1. Physical science that explains how a helium balloon rises

   (chisspy) _____

2. The amount of material in a tree

   (sams) _____

3. Anything that has mass and takes up space

   (tarmet) _____

4. Physical science that explains how acid rain forms

   (therycism) _____

5. Study of things around you

   (salichpy niecesc) _____

6. What is needed to make things move

   (genery) _____

Directions Read the terms. Cross out the term that does not belong. Explain why the term does not belong.

7. organizing, tuning fork, predicting _____

8. technology, chemistry, physics _____

9. balance scale, Bunsen burner, measurements _____

10. matter, computers, microwave ovens _____

Systems of Measurement

Directions The table describes some units of measurement. Each unit has a metric equivalent. Complete the table with the help of a dictionary or other reference tool. The first item is done for you.

Units of Measurement

Unit	Description	Equals (Metric)
1. knot	unit used to measure air and wind speed	about 1.9 kilometers per hour
2. carat	unit of weight for gemstones	
3. hand	unit of length for measuring height of horses	
4. league	unit of distance in measuring land: about 3 miles	
5. light-year	unit of distance equal to the distance light travels through space in one year	
6. furlong	unit of distance in measuring land: 220 yards	
7. pound	unit of weight	
8. fathom	unit of length used to measure the depth of water	
9. cable	unit of length used at sea	
10. gallon	unit of liquid volume	
11. span	unit of length, based on the spread of fingers	
12. rod	unit of length for measuring land	
13. ell	unit for measuring cloth	
14. peck	unit of volume used to measure grains and fruit	
15. foot	unit of length	

Adding and Subtracting Metric Units of Length

Directions Add or subtract the numbers in each problem. Then simplify your answer. Write your answer on the line. The first one is done for you.

1.   12 centimeters 5 millimeters
    +   5 centimeters 3 millimeters   17 centimeters 8 millimeters

2.   10 meters 8 centimeters
    +   9 meters 9 centimeters   _____

3.   22 meters 4 centimeters
    +   3 meters 5 centimeters   _____

4.   20 meters 10 millimeters
    +   23 millimeters   _____

5.   10 centimeters 5 millimeters
    + 22 centimeters 8 millimeters   _____

6.   6 meters 2 centimeters
    +   4 meters   _____

7.   23 millimeters
    +   3 millimeters   _____

8.   11 meters 9 millimeters
    +   8 meters 6 millimeters   _____

9.   39 meters 9 millimeters
    −   1 meter 6 millimeters   _____

10.   20 meters 7 centimeters
    −   5 centimeters   _____

Using Metric Measurements to Find Area

Directions Use the formula to find the area of each figure.
Write your answer on the line. Include the unit in your answer.

area = length × width

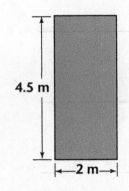

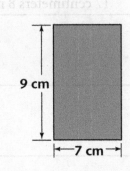

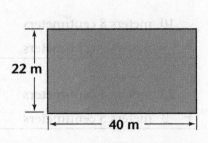

1. _____

2. _____

3. _____

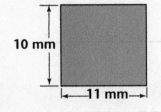

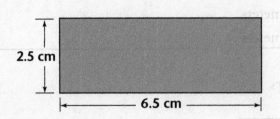

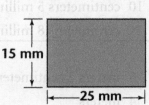

4. _____

5. _____

6. _____

Directions Write the missing number on the line. Be sure to include the unit in the answer.

7. 6 m × _____ = 48 m^2

8. 12 cm × 18 cm = _____

9. 14 mm × _____ = 1,400 mm^2

10. 120 m × 17 m = _____

11. 8.5 mm × 3.5 mm = _____

12. 35 m × 30 m = _____

13. 4 cm × _____ = 56 cm^2

14. 20 cm × 20 cm = _____

15. _____ × 70 m = 140 m^2

Name _____ Date _____ Period _____

Using Metric Measurements to Find Volume

Directions Use the formula to find the volume of each figure. Write your answer on the line. Include the unit in your answer.

volume = length × width × height

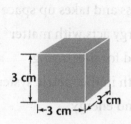

1. _____

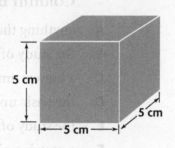

2. _____

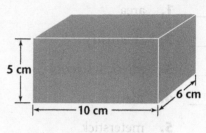

3. _____

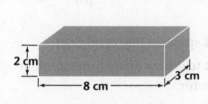

4. _____

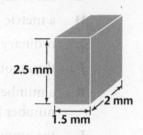

5. _____

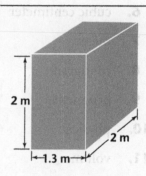

6. _____

Directions Write the volume of each box on the line. Be sure to include the unit in your answer.

7. 10 m × 10 m × 10 m = _____

8. 1.5 cm × 1.5 cm × 1.5 cm = _____

9. 4 mm × 4 mm × 4 mm = _____

10. 240 m × 2 m × 150 m = _____

11. 20 mm × 5 mm × 10 mm = _____

12. 40 cm × 15 cm × 10 cm = _____

13. 1.1 cm × 2 cm × 50 cm = _____

14. 2 m × 3 m × 2 m = _____

15. 225 cm × 150 cm × 50 cm = _____

The Metric System: Terms Review

Directions Match each term in Column A with its meaning in Column B.
Write the correct letter on the line.

Column A

____ 1. area
____ 2. chemistry
____ 3. physical science
____ 4. matter
____ 5. meterstick
____ 6. cubic centimeter
____ 7. meter
____ 8. centigram
____ 9. exponent
____ 10. physics
____ 11. volume
____ 12. metric system
____ 13. customary
____ 14. unit
____ 15. mass

Column B

A anything that has mass and takes up space
B the study of how energy acts with matter
C a known amount used for measuring
D the basic unit of length in the metric system
E the study of matter and energy
F a metric unit that means centimeter $\times$ centimeter $\times$ centimeter
G the study of matter and how it changes
H a metric unit of measure that is $\frac{1}{100}$ of a gram
I ordinary
J the amount of space an object takes up
K a number that tells how many times another number is a factor
L the amount of material an object has
M system of measurement used by scientists
N a common tool for measuring length in the metric system
O the amount of surface an object has

Directions Write the abbreviation of the word in bold on the line.

____ 16. There are 1,000 **milliliters** in a liter.
____ 17. 1,000 meters is equal to a **kilometer.**
____ 18. A **milligram** is $\frac{1}{1,000}$ of a gram.
____ 19. A **meter** is equal to about 39 inches.
____ 20. A **centigram** is $\frac{1}{100}$ of a gram.

____ 21. One **kilogram** is about 2.2 pounds.
____ 22. A **millimeter** is $\frac{1}{1,000}$ of a meter.
____ 23. The basic unit of mass in the metric system is the **gram.**
____ 24. A **liter** is slightly more than a quart.
____ 25. A **centimeter** is $\frac{1}{100}$ of a meter.

Properties of Objects

Directions Look at the objects below. On the lines, write properties that describe each object. Estimate each object's size, mass, and volume. Use the chart to help you choose units of measure.

	Volume of a Liquid	**Volume of a Solid**	**Mass**
Measured in	mL (milliliters) L (liters)	cm^3 (cubic centimeters) m^3 (cubic meters)	g (grams) kg (kilograms)
Examples	individual carton of milk is 237 mL water bottle is 500 mL	textbook is 1,500 cm^3	textbook is 1 kg

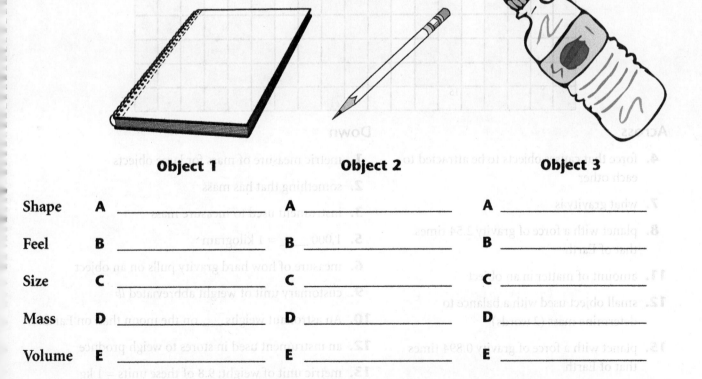

	Object 1	**Object 2**	**Object 3**
Shape	A _____	A _____	A _____
Feel	B _____	B _____	B _____
Size	C _____	C _____	C _____
Mass	D _____	D _____	D _____
Volume	E _____	E _____	E _____

Mass and Weight

Directions   Use the clues to complete the crossword puzzle. You may also use your book for help.

Across

4. force that causes objects to be attracted to each other

7. what gravity is

8. planet with a force of gravity 2.54 times that of Earth

11. amount of matter in an object

12. small object used with a balance to determine mass (2 words)

15. planet with a force of gravity 0.894 times that of Earth

Down

1. metric measure of mass for large objects

2. something that has mass

3. instrument used to measure mass

5. 1,000 ____ = 1 kilogram

6. measure of how hard gravity pulls on an object

9. customary unit of weight abbreviated *lb*

10. An astronaut weighs ___ on the moon than on Earth.

12. an instrument used in stores to weigh produce

13. metric unit of weight; 9.8 of these units = 1 kg

14. planet with a moon named Deimos

Measuring the Mass of a Liquid

Directions You want to buy perfume or cologne. How much product is in a bottle? That depends on the mass of the liquid in the bottle. Find the mass of the liquid in each bottle. Then find the cost per gram of the product. Divide the price by the mass of the liquid to find the cost per gram.

EXAMPLE A bottle has 20 grams of perfume. The bottle of perfume costs $45.00.

Cost per gram = $\dfrac{\$45.00}{20 \text{ grams}}$

Cost per gram = $2.25

Name	Mass of Empty Bottle	Mass of Filled Bottle	Mass of Perfume or Cologne	Cost per Gram
Tidal	82 g	125 g	**1.**	**2.**
Freesia	55 g	85 g	**3.**	**4.**
Daisy	66 g	92 g	**5.**	**6**
Breeze	70 g	150 g	**7.**	**8.**
Roma	80 g	130g	**9.**	**10.**

11. Which perfume costs the most per gram? _____

12. Which costs the least per gram? _____

13. Which costs more per gram: Tidal or Breeze? _____

14. List the perfumes in order, from most expensive per gram to least expensive.

_____

_____

15. What else besides price would you consider when buying perfume or cologne?

_____

_____

Measuring the Volume of Liquid

Directions Use the terms in the box to complete each sentence. Write your answer on the line. You will use some terms more than once.

bottom	laboratory	scale
cubic centimeter	level	spaces
divide	meniscus	subtract
graduated cylinder	milliliters	volume

1. Liquid volume is measured in cubic centimeters or _____.

2. In the _____, scientists use milliliters to measure the volume of liquid.

3. The largest _____ usually holds one liter of liquid.

4. One milliliter has the same volume as one _____.

5. You read the volume of a liquid by looking at the _____ on a graduated cylinder.

Procedure A: Measure with a Graduated Cylinder

6. Pour liquid into a _____.

7. Place yourself so that your eyes are _____ with the top of liquid.

8. Look at the _____, the curved surface of the liquid.

9. Find the _____ of the curve of the liquid.

10. Read the _____ on the outside of the cylinder at this point.

Procedure B: Read the Scale on a Graduated Cylinder

11. The volume of a liquid is measured in _____.

12. Find out how many mL the _____ on the scale stand for.

13. Now _____ the numbers on any two long lines next to each other.

14. Count the spaces between the long lines and _____ this number into the answer from step 13.

15. This will give you the _____ represented by each line.

Comparing and Contrasting Objects

Directions When you compare things or ideas, you tell how they are alike. When you contrast them, you tell how they are different. Compare and contrast each pair of words.

How They Are Alike	How They Are Different

1. length—volume: _____

_____

_____

2. cube—sphere: _____

_____

_____

3. regular shapes—irregular shapes: _____

_____

_____

4. balance—graduated cylinder: _____

_____

_____

5. liquid mass—liquid volume: _____

_____

_____

Directions Tell how you would measure the volume of each item.
Write *formula* or *displacement of water method* on the line.

6. a cement block _____

7. a stone _____

8. a golf ball _____

9. a refrigerator box _____

10. a game die _____

The Properties of Matter: Terms Review

Directions Match each term in Column A with its meaning in Column B.
Write the correct letter on the line.

Column A		Column B
_____ **1.** weight	**A**	a characteristic that helps identify an object
_____ **2.** newton	**B**	the measure of how hard gravity pulls on an object
_____ **3.** meniscus		
_____ **4.** standard mass	**C**	an instrument used to measure mass
_____ **5.** balance	**D**	method of measuring volume of irregularly shaped object
_____ **6.** property		
_____ **7.** density	**E**	a round cylinder used to measure the volume of a liquid
_____ **8.** graduated cylinder	**F**	the curved surface of a liquid
_____ **9.** displacement of water	**G**	the metric unit of weight
	H	a measure of how tightly matter is packed into a given volume
	I	small object used with a balance to determine mass

Directions Unscramble the word or words in parentheses to complete each
sentence. Write the answer on the line.

10. Length times width times height equals _____. (lumove)

11. Use a _____ to measure mass. (canebla)

12. Measure the volume of a liquid using a _____. (dateargud dinecrly)

13. Read the bottom of the curve of the _____
in a graduated cylinder. (misscenu)

14. A mass of 1 kg has a metric weight of 9.8 _____. (swetonn)

15. To measure the volume of a stone, you could use the _____
of water method. (palstendicem)

Identifying Solids, Liquids, and Gases

Directions Each figure below represents a different state of matter. Use the figures to complete the following statements.

1. What are the smallest particles of a substance that have the same properties as the substance?

   They are _____.

2. Liquids are best represented by Figure _____.

3. Gases are best represented by Figure _____.

4. Figure _____ shows the state of matter with the greatest density.

5. One state of matter that is not represented by the figures is _____.

Figure A

Figure B

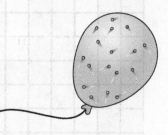

Figure C

Directions Match each item with the figure that best represents it. Write the letter of the figure on the line.

6. ice cube _____

7. skateboard _____

8. feather _____

9. helium in a balloon _____

10. raindrop _____

11. old ring _____

12. orange juice _____

13. bar of soap _____

14. air _____

15. water vapor from a cooking pot _____

What Are Elements?

Directions Read the clues to complete the crossword puzzle. Each word is related to elements.

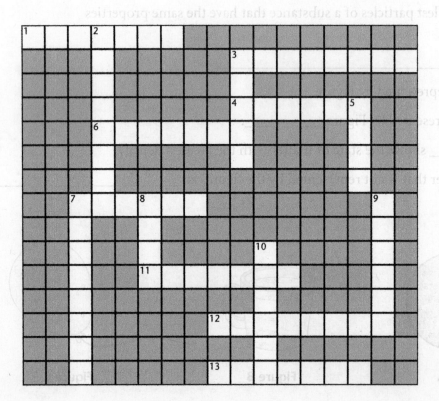

Across

1. matter that has only one kind of atom

3. an element used to make soft-drink cans

4. A water molecule contains one of these atoms.

6. an element that keeps bones healthy

7. an element used in some balloons

11. There are 92 of these elements.

12. an element used in fertilizers

13. an element used in thermometers

Down

2. A water _____ is made of three parts.

3. All of these are alike in the same element.

5. an element used in signs

7. There are two of these atoms in a water molecule.

8. one of the elements in steel

9. A pencil point has billions of these atoms.

10. takes up space and has mass

What Are Compounds?

Directions Use the terms in the box to complete each sentence.

carbon
compound
gases
hydrogen
laboratory
liquid
salt
sodium
sugar
water

1. A _____ is formed when two or more atoms of different elements join together.

2. The compound formed from two atoms of hydrogen and one atom of oxygen is _____.

3. Oxygen and hydrogen are _____, but when combined they form a _____.

4. A compound used for cooking made from sodium and chlorine is _____.

5. Baking soda is a compound made of _____, _____, _____, and oxygen.

6. To find out if a substance is an element or a compound, test it in a _____.

7. A compound used for cooking made of carbon, hydrogen, and oxygen is _____.

Directions When you compare and contrast things, you tell how they are alike and how they are different. Answer these questions by comparing and/or contrasting.

8. How are an element and a compound alike and different?

_____

_____

9. How are water and hydrogen different?

_____

_____

10. How are sugar and baking soda alike?

_____

_____

What Are Atoms Like?

Directions Label the model with letters *e*, *n*, and *p* to show its parts. The letter *e* stands for electron, *n* for neutron, and *p* for proton. Then complete each sentence about the model by writing an answer on the line.

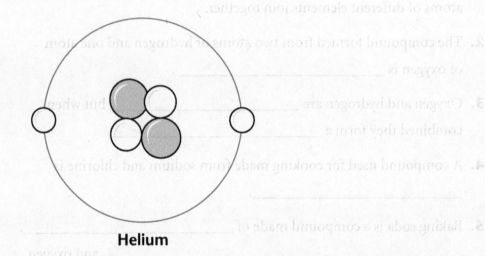

Helium

1. The model shows (a, an) _____ of helium.

2. The nucleus consists of _____

   and _____.

3. The particles labeled *p* are _____.

4. The particles labeled *e* are _____.

5. The particles labeled *n* are _____.

Directions Complete the chart.

Element	Number of Protons	Number of Electrons
6. lithium	3	
7. boron		5
8. carbon		6
9. oxygen	8	
10. neon	10	

The Structure of Matter: Terms Review

Directions Match each term in Column A with its meaning in Column B.
Write the letter on the line.

Column A		Column B	
_____ 1.	molecule	**A**	a particle found in the nucleus of an atom
_____ 2.	electron	**B**	a particle with a negative charge
_____ 3.	atom	**C**	the form that matter has
_____ 4.	gas	**D**	the form of matter with no definite shape or volume
_____ 5.	neutron	**E**	the building block of matter
_____ 6.	state of matter	**F**	the smallest particle of a substance that has its properties
_____ 7.	liquid		
_____ 8.	model	**G**	the form of matter with a definite volume but not definite shape
_____ 9.	nucleus	**H**	the central part of an atom
		I	something made to show how something else works

Directions Unscramble the letters in parentheses to make a word that completes
each sentence. Write the word on the line.

10. A _____ is a substance made of two or more
elements combined chemically. (modoncup)

11. A _____ is a particle with a positive charge in
the nucleus of an atom.   (troonp)

12. A very hot gas made of charged particles is _____. (amalps)

13. The form of matter with a definite shape and volume is a _____. (doils)

Directions Write an answer to each question.

14. How do the mass number and the atomic number of an element differ?

_____

15. How are natural elements different from other elements?

_____

Words from Chemical Symbols

Directions Read the clue in Column A. You can find the answer from the elements in Column B. In Column C, write the symbols for the elements in Column B. The word you form should be the correct answer for the clue. The first one is done for you.

A	B	C
1. A farm animal	cobalt-tungsten	CoW
2. A musical group	barium-neodymium	_____
3. The opposite of *lose*	tungsten-iodine-nitrogen	_____
4. A building material	bromine-iodine-carbon-potassium	_____
5. Found on a door	potassium-nitrogen-oxygen-boron	_____
6. Used to write on a blackboard	carbon-hydrogen-aluminum-potassium	_____
7. A dog's sound	boron-argon-potassium	_____
8. It's 150 million km away	sulfur-uranium-nitrogen	_____
9. A source of energy	cobalt-aluminum	_____
10. A funny person	chlorine-oxygen-tungsten-nitrogen	_____
11. Used in hockey	plutonium-carbon-potassium	_____
12. Something to run in	radium-cerium	_____
13. A form of money	cobalt-iodine-nitrogen	_____
14. Show of affection	potassium-iodine-sulfur-sulfur	_____
15. Another word for *ill*	silicon-carbon-potassium	_____
16. An infant	barium-boron-yttrium	_____
17. A narrow street	lanthanum-neon	_____
18. To make better	helium-aluminum	_____
19. King of the beasts	lithium-oxygen-nitrogen	_____
20. A form of precipitation	radium-iodine-nitrogen	_____

Name _____ Date _____ Period _____

Using the Periodic Table

Directions Write the atomic number for the element in each square. Then add the five atomic numbers in each row and in each column. Write the sums. If your atomic numbers are correct, the sums will all be the same.

Fe	As	Ne	Cl	Cr	Sums
___	___	___	___	___	___
Ge	Si	S	V	Mn	
___	___	___	___	___	___
Al	P	Ti	Cu	Ga	
___	___	___	___	___	___
K	Sc	Ni	Zn	Mg	
___	___	___	___	___	___
Ca	Co	Se	Na	Ar	
___	___	___	___	___	___

Sums

Classifying Elements: Terms Review

Directions Match each term in Column A with its meaning in Column B.
Write the correct letter on the line.

Column A		Column B
_____ **1.** periodic table	**A**	an element that conducts heat and electricity and can be shaped
_____ **2.** alloy		
_____ **3.** nonmetal	**B**	one of a group of gases that do not react with other substances under ordinary circumstances
_____ **4.** atomic mass	**C**	a group of elements with similar properties arranged in a column on the periodic table
_____ **5.** deuterium		
_____ **6.** isotope	**D**	the average mass of all the isotopes of an element
_____ **7.** noble gas	**E**	an arrangement of elements by increasing atomic number
_____ **8.** family		
_____ **9.** inert	**F**	a mixture of two or more metals
_____**10.** metal	**G**	one of a group of elements found on the right side of the periodic table, which are not good conductors of heat or electricity
	H	form of an element that has the same number of protons and electrons but a different number of neutrons
	I	a form of hydrogen
	J	lacking the power to move

Directions Unscramble the word in parentheses to complete each sentence.

11. A(n) _____ is an abbreviation for the name of an element.   (mobsly)

12. A(n)_____ is one of a group of elements placed on the left side of the periodic table. It is usually shiny and a good conductor of electricity and heat.   (altem)

13. Under ordinary circumstances, _____ gases will not combine with other substances.   (entir)

14. The isotope of hydrogen that has one proton and two neutrons is _____.   (riimutt)

15. H-1, H-2, and H-3 are examples of _____.   (stoipoes)

Physical and Chemical Changes

Directions Read each change listed in items 1 through 15. Write each change in the table. If it is a physical change, write the change in the left column. If it is a chemical change, write the change in the right column.

Physical Change	Chemical Change

1. scrambling eggs in a bowl
2. a silver spoon tarnishing
3. a puddle drying up
4. chopping onions
5. a copper roof turning green
6. water drops forming on the outside of a glass
7. bread baking

8. paper burning
9. picking tomatoes from a plant
10. mixing baking soda and vinegar
11. snow falling
12. painting a room
13. car-exhaust fumes mixing with water
14. adding a drink powder to water
15. bike spokes rusting

Directions How are physical changes and chemical changes different? Write your answer below.

_____

_____

_____

Energy Levels

Directions Write your answers on the lines.

1. How many electrons does the K level of an atom hold? _____

2. How many electrons does the L level of an atom hold? _____

3. How many electrons does the M level of an atom hold? _____

4. How many electrons does the N level of an atom hold? _____

5. What is the total number of electrons the four levels will hold? _____

6. A hydrogen atom has 1 electron. In which level is it? _____

7. A magnesium atom has 12 electrons. To what level are its electrons found? _____

8. A zinc atom has 30 electrons. To what level are its electrons found? _____

9. A nitrogen atom has 7 electrons. To what level are its electrons found? _____

10. A sulfur atom has 16 electrons. To what level are its electrons found? _____

11. A lithium atom has 3 electrons. To what level are its electrons found? _____

12. An iron atom has 26 electrons. To what level are its electrons found? _____

13. A mercury atom has 80 electrons. To what level are its electrons found? _____

14. A zirconium atom has 40 electrons. To what level are its electrons found? _____

15. A californium atom has 98 electrons. To what level are its electrons found? _____

Directions Draw a magnesium atom. Show its energy levels and electrons.

Working with Chemical Formulas

Directions Write the chemical formula for each compound described. You ___
the periodic table on pages 100–101 to find the chemical symbols.

1. silver chloride = one atom of silver + one atom of chlorine

_____

2. hydrochloric acid = one atom of hydrogen + one atom of chlorine

_____

3. hydrogen peroxide = two atoms of hydrogen + two atoms of oxygen

_____

4. magnesium carbonate = one atom of magnesium + one atom of carbon + three atoms of oxygen

_____

5. glucose = six atoms of carbon + twelve atoms of hydrogen + six atoms of oxygen

_____

6. lead nitrate = one atom of lead + two nitrate radicals

_____

Directions Complete the table. Write the names of the elements in each
compound. Then write the number of atoms in each element.

Compound	Elements	Atoms
7. potassium chloride, KCl		
8. sucrose, $C_{12}H_{22}O_{11}$		
9. ammonium bromide, NH_4Br		
10. ammonium carbonate, $(NH_4)_2CO_3$		

Matching Chemical Formulas with Chemical Names

Directions Compounds have a chemical formula and a chemical name. Draw a line to match each formula in the left column with the correct name in the right column. You can use the periodic table on pages 100–101 to help you with this activity.

Column 1	Column 2
1. NaF	beryllium oxide
2. $MgCl_2$	potassium iodide
3. AgBr	silver chloride
4. LiOH	sodium fluoride
5. KCl	silver sulfide
6. LiF	beryllium chloride
7. BeO	lithium chloride
8. KI	gallium arsenide
9. $BeCl_2$	strontium chlorate
10. $FeCO_3$	lithium hydroxide
11. Ag_2S	magnesium chloride
12. $Sr(ClO_3)_2$	silver bromide
13. LiCl	iron carbonate
14. GaAs	potassium chloride
15. AgCl	lithium fluoride

Compounds: Terms Review

Directions Read the clues. Write the answers in the puzzle.

Across

3. water freezing into ice: a _____ change

5. has sour taste

7. examples: OH, SO_4, NO_3

8. electrons can fill this up (2 words)

10. shorthand for chemical compound: a chemical _____

12. an atom that has a charge

13. metallic element, symbol is Pb

14. small digit, indicates number of atoms

15. litmus paper is one

Down

1. scale for measuring acids and bases

2. contains two elements (2 words)

4. has bitter taste

6. wood burning to ashes: a _____ change

9. attractive force between atoms: a chemical _____

11. this metal turns green if exposed to oxygen

Reactions and Solutions

Directions Write the best word for each description on the line.

1. person who tried to change various substances into gold _____

2. chemical change _____

3. part of a solution in which a substance dissolves _____

4. to break apart _____

5. a mixture in which one substance is dissolved in another _____

6. what you must apply to cause some chemical reactions _____

7. combination of substances in which no reaction occurs _____

8. what elements do in a reaction _____

9. the substance that is dissolved in a solution _____

10. what sugar breaks into when it is dissolved in water _____

Directions Write the answer to each question.

11. What is the difference between a mixture and a solution?

_____

_____

12. What is the difference between a solute and a solvent?

_____

_____

13. What is the difference between a mixture and a chemical reaction?

_____

_____

14. Name an example of a gas dissolved in a liquid.

_____

15. Name an example of a solution with a liquid solute and a solid solvent.

_____

Using Chemical Equations to Show Reactions

Directions Read the clues and complete the puzzle.

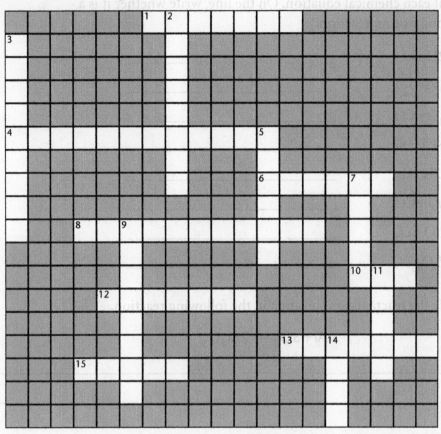

Across

1. something formed by a reaction

4. The law of _____ of matter states that matter cannot be created or destroyed in a chemical change.

6. this cannot be created or destroyed in a chemical reaction

8. a number before a formula in a chemical equation

10. This makes a statement about what happens in a reaction.

12. to keep the number of atoms the same on both sides of an equation

13. These are found in chemical equations along with chemical formulas and numbers.

15. These are rearranged during a reaction.

Down

2. shown on the left side of a chemical equation

3. In $2H_2O$, the number before H_2O tells how many _____.

5. A coefficient is one.

7. In a balanced equation, the number of atoms on both sides are _____.

9. a statement that uses symbols, formulas, and numbers

11. a symbol that stands for "yields" or "makes"

14. this does not change during a reaction

Synthesis and Decomposition Reactions

Directions Look at each chemical equation. On the line, write whether it is a synthesis or a decomposition reaction.

1. $2H_2 + O_2 \rightarrow 2H_2O$ _____

2. $2MgO \rightarrow 2Mg + O_2$ _____

3. $H_2CO_3 \rightarrow H_2O + CO_2$ _____

4. $2KClO_3 \rightarrow 2KCl + 3O_2$ _____

5. $4Fe + 3O_2 \rightarrow 2Fe2O_3$ _____

6. $CaCO_3 \rightarrow CaO + CO_2$ _____

7. $2PbO_2 \rightarrow 2PbO + O_2$ _____

8. $4P + 5O_2 \rightarrow P_4O_{10}$ _____

Directions Identify the reactants and product in the following reaction.

$$4Al + 3O_2 \rightarrow 2Al_2O_3$$

9. reactants _____

10. product _____

Directions Use the following chemical equation to answer questions 11–15.

$$2Cu + O_2 \rightarrow 2CuO$$

11. What are the reactants? _____

12. What is the product? _____

13. How many atoms of copper are on both sides of the equation? _____

14. How many atoms of oxygen are on both sides of the equation? _____

15. What type of reaction is this? _____

How Matter Changes: Terms Review

Directions Match each term in Column A with its meaning in Column B.
Write the correct letter on the line.

Column A

_____ **1.** dissolve

_____ **2.** mixture

_____ **3.** reactant

_____ **4.** coefficient

_____ **5.** chemical reaction

_____ **6.** chemical equation

_____ **7.** solute

_____ **8.** balance

Column B

A a chemical change in which elements are combined or rearranged

B to make the number of atoms the same on both sides of a chemical equation

C a statement that uses symbols and formulas to describe a chemical reaction

D a substance that dissolves in a solution

E a substance that changes in a chemical reaction

F a number placed before a chemical formula to show the number of molecules

G a combination of substances in which there is no reaction

H to break apart

Directions Unscramble the word or words in parentheses to complete each sentence below.

9. A _____ is a solid that is formed in a reaction and sinks
to the bottom of a solution. (tiptreepaic)

10. A _____ is the substance in which a solute dissolves. (novlest)

11. A _____ is one kind of mixture. (oilsnout)

12. The law of _____ of matter states that matter cannot
be created or destroyed. (introvosance)

13. A _____ is a substance that is formed during a reaction
and shown on the right side of a chemical equation. (cuptrod)

Directions Write your answers to these questions on the lines.

14. How do a single-replacement reaction and a double-replacement reaction differ?

_____

_____

15. How do a synthesis reaction and a decomposition reaction differ?

_____

_____

Calculating Speed

EXAMPLE To calculate average speed, divide the distance traveled by the elapsed time.

$$\text{average speed} = \frac{\text{distance}}{\text{time}}$$

distance = 550 miles
elapsed time = 10 hours
average speed = 55 mi/hr

Directions Calculate the average speed. Write the answer on the line.

1. distance = 120 millimeters _____
time = 60 seconds

2. distance = 400 meters _____
time = 80 seconds

3. distance = 700 centimeters _____
time = 35 seconds

4. distance = 1,000 meters _____
time = 100 seconds

5. distance = 175 miles _____
time = 5 hours

6. distance = 12.5 millimeters _____
time = 0.5 seconds

7. distance = 0.045 meters _____
time = 0.5 seconds

8. distance = 0.015 millimeters _____
time = 0.10 seconds

9. distance = 966 yards _____
time = 42 seconds

10. distance = 396 kilometers _____
time = 6 hours

Directions Read each word problem. Write the answer on the line.

11. If a runner goes 200 meters in 50 seconds, what is her average speed? _____

12. If a train goes 846 miles in 9 hours, what is its average speed? _____

13. A marathon runner can go 6 miles per hour. How long will it take
him to run 26 miles? _____

14. An airplane traveled for 5 hours at an average speed of 450 miles
per hour. How far did it go? _____

15. A car can average 52 miles per hour. How long will it take to go 416 miles? _____

Using a Graph to Describe Motion

Directions Use the data in the table to complete the graph below. Plot the distance traveled for each of the three vehicles. Then answer the questions.

Elapsed Time in Hours	Distance Traveled in Kilometers		
	Car	Motorcycle	Train
1	75	25	50
2	150	50	100
3	225	75	150
4	300	100	200
5	375	125	250

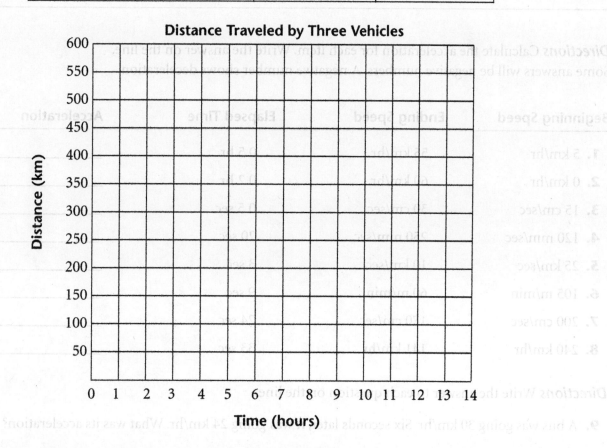

Distance Traveled by Three Vehicles

1. How would you describe the motion of all three vehicles? _____

2. How far would each vehicle travel in 6 hours at the same speed? _____

Acceleration

EXAMPLE To calculate acceleration, first subtract the beginning speed from the ending speed to find the change in speed. Then divide the change in speed by the time it takes to make the change.

beginning speed = 50 km/hr
ending speed = 65 km/hr
elapsed time = 5 sec
acceleration = 3 km/hr per sec

Step 1 65 km/hr − 50 km/hr = 15 km/hr

$$acceleration = \frac{change\ in\ speed}{change\ in\ time}$$

Step 2 3 km/hr per sec = $\frac{15\ km/hr}{5\ sec}$

Directions Calculate the acceleration for each item. Write the answer on the line. Some answers will be negative numbers. A negative number shows deceleration.

Beginning Speed	Ending Speed	Elapsed Time	Acceleration
1. 5 km/hr	55 km/hr	0.5 hr	_____
2. 0 km/hr	60 km/hr	0.2 hr	_____
3. 15 cm/sec	30 cm/sec	0.5 sec	_____
4. 120 mm/sec	250 mm/sec	20 sec	_____
5. 25 km/sec	10 km/sec	3 sec	_____
6. 105 m/min	60 m/min	9 sec	_____
7. 200 cm/sec	170 cm/sec	24 sec	_____
8. 240 km/hr	141 km/hr	33 sec	_____

Directions Write the answer to each question on the line.

9. A bus was going 30 km/hr. Six seconds later, it was going 24 km/hr. What was its acceleration?

_____

10. A bicycle was going 48 meters per minute. Five minutes earlier it was going 40 meters per minute. What was its acceleration?

_____

The Laws of Motion

Directions Read the clues. Then complete the puzzle.

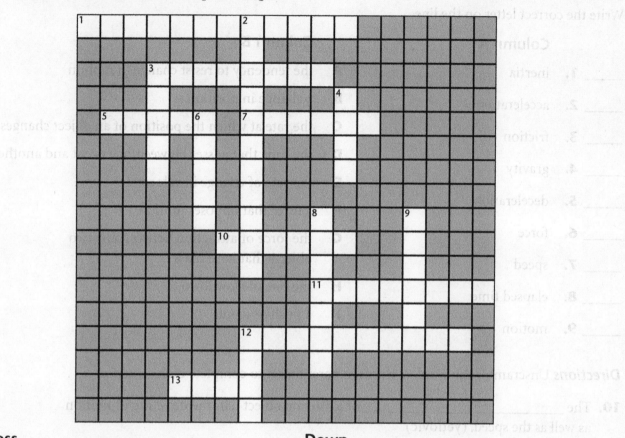

Across

1. force = mass × _____

3. a force that opposes motion

5. The _____ law of motion states that if no force acts on an object at rest, it will remain at rest.

7. This is a change in position.

10. The _____ law of motion describes the amount of force needed to change the motion of an object.

11. For every action, there is an equal and opposite _____.

12. One form of friction is air _____.

13. The amount of force needed to accelerate an object depends on the object's _____.

Down

2. Designers work to reduce air resistance on these.

3. a push or a pull

4. Friction is created when things slide or _____ over each other.

6. The _____ law of motion tells what happens when one object exerts a force on a second object.

8. the tendency of an object to resist changes in its motion

9. the scientist who proposed three laws to explain motion

12. If no force acts on a nonmoving object, it remains at _____.

Motion: Terms Review

Directions Match each term in Column A with its meaning in Column B.
Write the correct letter on the line.

Column A	Column B
_____ **1.** inertia	**A** the tendency to resist change in motion
_____ **2.** acceleration	**B** a change in position
_____ **3.** friction	**C** the rate at which the position of an object changes
_____ **4.** gravity	**D** the time that passes between one event and another
_____ **5.** deceleration	**E** the rate of change in velocity
_____ **6.** force	**F** a force that opposes motion
_____ **7.** speed	**G** the force of attraction between any two objects that have mass
_____ **8.** elapsed time	**H** the rate of slowdown
_____ **9.** motion	**I** a push or a pull

Directions Unscramble the word or words in parentheses to complete each sentence.

10. The _____ of a moving object tells the direction of motion
as well as the speed. (yetlovic)

11. A _____ has no acceleration. (cannotts deeps)

12. The length of the path between two points is _____. (candetis)

13. The law of _____ states that gravity depends on
mass and distance. (savenuril tatairoving)

Directions Tell how each pair is alike and different.

14. speed and velocity

_____

_____

15. inertia and friction

_____

_____

What Is Work?

Directions On the line, write the word or words that best complete the sentence.

1. When work is done, an object changes its _____.

2. Work is done when a force moves an object in the _____ of the force that is applied.

3. To measure work, you must _____ the force by the distance through which it acts.

4. Work is measured in newton-meters, or _____.

5. The formula for measuring work is _____.

Directions Use the formula *work = force × distance* to find each answer. Give the answer in joules.

6. Julie rolled a 2-kg ball down a ramp 10 meters long. (Remember, 1 kg = 9.8 newtons.) How much work was done? _____

7. Kevin lifted a 10-newton box a distance of 1.5 meters. How much work did he do? _____

8. A high jumper weighing 700 newtons jumps over a bar 2.0 meters high. What work does the high jumper do? _____

9. A mountain climber who weighs 900 newtons scales a 100-meter cliff. How much work does the climber do? _____

10. A parent uses a force of 300 newtons to pull a toddler in a wagon for 400 meters. How much work did the parent do? _____

11. Pushing a lawn mower requires a force of 200 newtons. If 4,000 joules of work is performed, how far has the mower moved? _____

12. A force of 550 newtons was used to move a stone 23 meters. How much work was done? _____

13. A box was pushed 42 meters, and 13,734 joules of work was done. How much force was used? _____

14. A child uses a 2-newton force to pull a wagon. He does 330 joules of work. How far did he pull the wagon? _____

15. A landscape worker attempted to move a 300 kg boulder for 30 minutes but was unable to budge it. How much work did the worker do? _____

Understanding Power

Directions Choose the word or words from the box that best complete each sentence.

force
joules
kilowatts
power
rate
second
watt
watts

1. Power is a measure of the _____ at which you do work.

2. Work measures the amount of _____ used to move an object a certain distance.

3. Work divided by time equals _____.

4. The units of measure for power are _____ per _____, or _____.

5. A _____ is 1 joule of work done in 1 second.

6. Usually, power is measured in _____, or 1,000-watt units.

Directions Use the formula to find each answer.

$$power = \frac{work}{time}$$

7. Alex pushed a stroller 2 blocks in 3 minutes. Then he pushed it 2 more blocks in 2 minutes. When did he use more power?

_____

8. How much power would it take to move a chair 5 meters in 15 seconds using a force of 51 newtons?

_____

9. A man can use a snowblower to move snow in 5 minutes. If he moves it with a shovel, it will take 20 minutes. He will use more power with which process?

_____

10. A tow truck uses a 600-newton force to pull a car for 10 meters. If it does this in 2 seconds, what is the tow truck's power?

_____

Understanding Energy

Directions Use the clues to complete the puzzle.

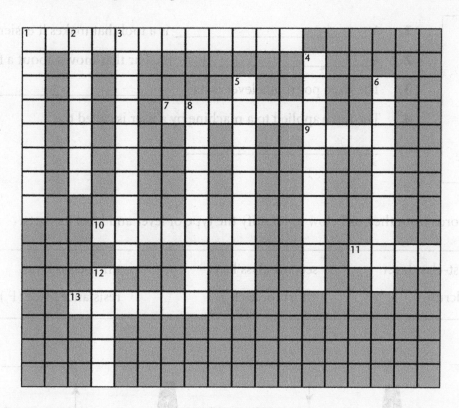

Across

1. The law of _____ of energy states that energy is neither created nor destroyed.

7. energy of motion

9. form of energy in matter, associated with movement of particles

10. form of energy received from the sun

11. the unit used to measure power

13. Work is measured in metric units called _____.

Down

1. form of energy a battery stores

2. form of energy released from the nucleus of an atom

3. form of energy that causes electrons to flow

4. form of energy in moving objects

5. machine for changing mechanical energy to electrical energy

6. stored energy

8. As an object falls, its kinetic energy _____.

12. amount of work done in a given amount of time

Using Levers

Directions Choose the word or words from the Word Bank that best complete each sentence.

Word Bank
effort force
fulcrum
lever
simple machine

1. A _____ is a tool that makes it easier to do work.

2. A _____ is a bar that moves about a fixed point.

3. The fixed point of a lever is its _____.

4. The force applied to a machine by a user is called the

_____.

Directions Use words from the box below to identify the type of lever and label its parts.

first-class lever	second-class lever	third-class lever
fulcrum	effort force (F$_e$)	resistance force (F$_r$)

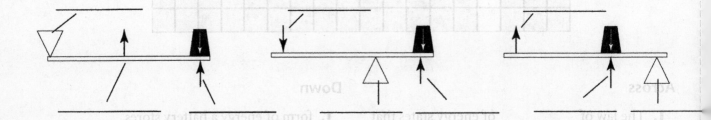

5. _____

6. _____

7. _____

Directions Use the following information to calculate work input, work output, and efficiency of the lever.

A worker presses on a lever with 250 newtons of force to lift a cart. His end of the lever moves 1.5 meters. The cart has a resistance of 430 newtons and moves 0.5 meter.

8. Work input of the lever: _____

9. Work output of the lever: _____

10. Efficiency of the lever: _____

Mechanical Advantage

Directions On the line, write the word or words that best complete each sentence.

1. The mechanical advantage is the number of times a machine multiplies the

   _____.

2. To increase the mechanical advantage of a lever, move the fulcrum closer to the
   _____ and farther from the _____.

3. The mechanical advantage of a machine is the resistance force _____
   by the effort force.

Directions Use the formula below to find the mechanical advantage (MA) of each
lever. Then answer the questions.

$$MA = \frac{\text{effort arm}}{\text{resistance arm}}$$

4. MA = _____   Lever A

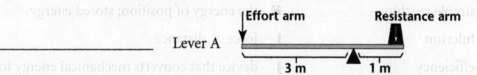

5. MA = _____   Lever B

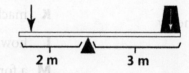

6. MA = _____   Lever C

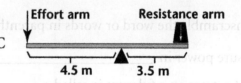

7. MA = _____   Lever D

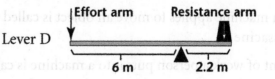

8. Write the formula for MA. _____

9. How would you increase MA? _____

   _____

10. What does MA show? _____

    _____

Work and Machines: Terms Review

Directions Match each term in Column A with its meaning in Column B.
Write the correct letter on the line.

Column A	Column B
____ 1. power	**A** wheel with a rope, chain, or belt around it
____ 2. joule	**B** fixed point around which a lever turns
____ 3. wheel and axle	**C** the energy of motion
____ 4. generator	**D** amount of work done in a given time
____ 5. screw	**E** tool with few parts that makes work easier
____ 6. energy	**F** the metric unit of work
____ 7. potential energy	**G** the ability to do work
____ 8. simple machine	**H** the energy of position; stored energy
____ 9. fulcrum	**I** force × distance
____ 10. efficiency	**J** device that converts mechanical energy to electrical energy
____ 11. pulley	
____ 12. kinetic energy	**K** machine made of a wheel attached to a shaft
____ 13. work	**L** how well a machine performs; work output/work input
	M a form of an inclined plane

Directions Unscramble the word or words in parentheses to complete each sentence.

14. You measure power in _____, or joules/second. (stwat)

15. A bar that rotates on a fulcrum is called a _____. (vreel)

16. The force a machine applies to move an object is called the _____ force. (tressacine)

17. The amount of work a person puts into a machine is called the _____. (kwor puint)

18. The amount of work a machine does against a resistance is called the
_____. (krwo puutto)

19. The number of times a machine multiplies your effort force is called its
_____. (acmehnlaic vnageadta)

20. A simple machine made of a ramp is an _____. (diinnelc leapn)

What Is Heat?

Directions Use the clues to complete the crossword puzzle. You may use your book for help.

Across

1. a place from which heat energy comes (2 words)

4. a form of energy resulting from the motion of particles in matter

5. _____ shine because their atoms release nuclear energy.

7. _____ gases make a car's engine work.

9. the nuclear reaction that occurs when atoms are joined together

11. the earth's most important heat source

12. the heat source for a toaster

14. the size of the particles whose movement creates heat

Down

1. Rubbing your _____ together produces heat.

2. a machine that uses heated water to operate (2 words)

3. Heat is a form of _____.

6. Heat results from the _____ of atoms and molecules.

8. the reaction that occurs when an atom splits

10. the part of a steam engine that changes water to steam

13. The first steam engine was used as a _____.

How Heat Affects Matter

Directions Choose the word from the Word Bank that best completes each sentence. You will use one word twice.

Word Bank			
evaporates	condensation	expands	contracts

1. Matter generally _____ when you heat it.

2. Water _____ when you boil it.

3. That frost on your window is an example of _____.

4. Water _____ when it becomes ice.

5. When particles in matter move more slowly, the matter usually _____.

Directions Each sentence tells about a process that is occurring. Write the letter of the process that is occurring on the line.

A liquid to solid   **B** liquid to gas   **C** solid to liquid   **D** gas to liquid

_____ **6.** A can of a soft drink in the freezer bursts.

_____ **7.** The bathroom walls are covered with water after your shower.

_____ **8.** The water in the teakettle is bubbling.

_____ **9.** The rain puddle is getting smaller.

_____ **10.** The ice cream is running down the cone.

Directions Complete the following sentences.

11. Cold air cannot hold as much _____ as warm air.

12. Molecules in a _____ move more freely than in a liquid.

13. Bubbles in boiling water are made up of water _____.

14. In the _____ months, a metal bridge is likely to expand.

15. One familiar material that does not contract when it gets colder is _____.

Temperature

Directions Write the correct word for each definition on the line. To check your answers, find each vocabulary word in the puzzle below.

1. a type of energy caused by the motion of molecules _____
2. results from a change at the melting point _____
3. results from a change at the boiling point _____
4. a measure of the average motion of the molecules in a substance _____
5. a device that measures temperature _____
6. the temperature scale on which water boils at 212° _____
7. the temperature scale used for scientific work _____
8. the temperature at which a solid changes to a liquid (2 words) _____
9. what water does at 100°C _____
10. the unit for measuring temperature _____
11. what water does at 32°F _____
12. a substance commonly used in antifreeze _____
13. to change from °F to °C, or vice versa _____
14. what state a substance becomes at freezing point _____
15. a liquid metal sometimes used in thermometers _____

```
G  B  O  I  L  S  D  L  Q  V  N  P  S  O  E
Y  Z  Q  Q  W  E  R  J  K  K  C  C  L  R  V
H  T  H  K  O  I  B  I  S  E  T  U  U  M  C
N  I  E  E  I  S  L  F  L  A  I  T  R  E  O
B  E  A  I  A  R  N  S  P  A  A  T  R  L  N
I  H  C  G  K  T  I  S  H  R  A  N  H  T  V
Y  N  B  E  L  U  E  E  R  G  E  D  I  E
R  E  A  N  S  Z  Y  P  V  S  P  M  I  N  R
U  R  M  P  E  S  M  S  V  Y  C  F  I  G  T
C  H  J  E  G  E  D  O  A  X  U  R  O  P  N
R  A  R  L  T  A  B  L  A  L  C  O  H  O  L
E  F  C  E  G  J  D  I  U  Q  I  L  L  I  U
M  A  F  S  M  Q  C  D  O  X  W  B  A  N  C
T  T  H  E  R  M  O  M  E  T  E  R  T  T  L
A  E  H  W  U  V  F  N  I  L  F  B  V  R  N
```

How to Measure Heat

Directions Answer the following items.

1. Write two statements that are true about temperature.

   A _____

   B _____

2. Write two statements that are true about heat.

   A _____

   B _____

3. Which gives off more heat, a potato heated to 375°F or a 20-lb turkey heated to the same temperature? Explain your answer.

   _____

   _____

Directions Calculate calories using the formula below. Write your answers on the lines.

Heat = change in temperature × mass

How many calories are needed or given off when you . . .

4. heat 1 gram of water 1°C? _____

5. cool 5 grams of water from 12°C to 8°C? _____

6. raise the heat of 3 grams of water 5°C? _____

7. lower the heat of 1 gram of water 25°C? _____

8. warm 12 grams of water from 98°C to 99°C? _____

9. make 2 grams of water 7°C warmer? _____

10. cool 2 grams of water 1°C? _____

11. bring up the temperature of 25 grams of water 1°C? _____

12. bring down the temperature of 2 grams of water from 27°C to 19°C? _____

13. cool 5 grams of water 2°C? _____

14. raise the heat of 20 grams of water 25°C? _____

15. heat 3 grams of water 15°C? _____

Heat: Terms Review

Directions Match each term in Column A with its meaning in Column B.
Write the correct letter on the line.

Column A	Column B
_____ **1.** calorie	**A** to change from a liquid to a gas
_____ **2.** temperature	**B** a form of energy resulting from the motion of particles in matter
_____ **3.** degree	
_____ **4.** Fahrenheit scale	**C** temperature at which a solid changes into a liquid
_____ **5.** evaporate	**D** the reaction occurring when the nucleus of an atom splits
_____ **6.** melting point	**E** a measure of how fast an object's particles are moving
_____ **7.** nuclear fission	**F** a device that measures temperature
_____ **8.** freezing point	**G** the temperature scale in which water freezes at 0°
_____ **9.** Celsius scale	**H** the temperature at which a substance changes to a gas
_____ **10.** nuclear fusion	**I** a unit of measurement on a temperature scale
_____ **11.** thermometer	**J** the reaction occurring when atoms are joined together
_____ **12.** boiling point	**K** the temperature scale commonly used in the United States
_____ **13.** contract	**L** the amount of heat needed to raise the temperature of 1 g of water 1°C
_____ **14.** heat	**M** the temperature at which a liquid changes to a solid
	N to become smaller in size

Directions Unscramble the word in parentheses to complete each sentence.

15. The flow of heat energy through matter by molecules bumping into

each other is _____. (noitcudonc)

16. Copper is an excellent _____ of heat energy. (rotnocduc)

17. Energy from the sun reaches us by _____. (idiotrana)

18. Warm liquids rise as a result of _____. (nevoncocit)

19. A _____ is space without matter. (camuvu)

20. A material that does not warm up or cool down quickly

is called an _____. (sularotin)

What Is Sound?

Directions Choose the term from the box that completes each sentence.

1. For a sound to occur, matter must _____, or move back and forth.

2. Vibration of an object causes _____ to compress and expand many times.

3. Air moves out in all directions from a vibrating object as a _____.

4. You may not see these waves, but you can hear the resulting _____.

5. Sounds grow fainter over distance because the sound waves become _____ the farther they travel from the vibrating object.

molecules
sound wave
sounds
vibrate
weaker

Directions Look at the figures below. Write a sentence or two that explains how the movement of the wire spring is like sound waves.

_____

_____

_____

Directions Write the answer to the question on the lines.

You toss a stone into water, and ripples spread out from where it hits. How are these ripples like sound waves?

_____

_____

_____

Different Sounds

Directions Each phrase tells something about intensity or frequency.
Write *intensity* or *frequency* beside each phrase.

_____ **1.** determines the volume (how loud or soft a sound is)

_____ **2.** determines the pitch (how high or low a sound is)

_____ **3.** measured in Hertz (Hz)

_____ **4.** measured in decibels

_____ **5.** related to amount of energy that sound waves have

_____ **6.** related to number of vibrations per second
                              (or number of cycles per second)

Directions Choose the word from the box that completes the sentence.

7. The frequency of a sound wave is measured in _____
    per second.

8. Sounds above 130 _____ can damage your hearing.

9. Volume is the way your _____ interpret
    intensity of a sound.

10. How high or low a sound seems is called its _____ .

11. Human ears can detect sounds with frequencies ranging from 20 to 20,000
    _____ .

cycles
decibels
ears
Hertz
pitch

Directions Label the parts of the sound wave using words from the Word Bank.

12. _____   **13.** _____

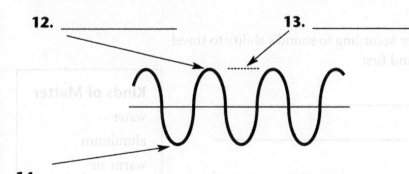

14. _____

15. _____

Word Bank

crest

1 cycle

trough

wavelength

How Sound Travels

Directions Write the answer to each question on the line.

1. Why can't sound travel through space? _____

_____

2. Why does sound travel fastest through solids? _____

_____

3. What is an echo? _____

_____

4. How are sonar and ultrasound alike? _____

_____

Directions Use what you know about the speed of sound to answer each question.

5. Lightning flashes in the distance. Seven seconds later, you hear the thunder.
   How far away is the storm?

_____

6. You yell into a canyon. You hear the echo in 3 seconds. How long did the sound of
   your voice travel before bouncing off a cliff?

_____

7. A ship sends out a sonar signal. The echo is heard after 6 seconds. How long did it take
   for the signal to reach the ocean bottom?

_____

Directions Put the kinds of matter in order according to sound's ability to travel
through them. List the fastest speed of sound first.

8. Sound travels fastest through _____.

9. Sound travels a little slower through _____.

10. Sound travels even slower through _____.

Kinds of Matter

water

aluminum

warm air

What Is Light?

Directions Choose the word or words from the box that best complete each sentence.

electromagnetic
empty space
light
photons
prism
visible spectrum

1. The sun is a major source of _____ on Earth.

2. Light is emitted from atoms in energy bundles called

   _____.

3. Light waves travel fastest through _____.

4. A _____ can separate white light into colors of the

   _____.

5. Waves that travel at the speed of light are called _____ waves.

Directions Write the colors of the visible spectrum in the order they appear. Then complete the sentence.

6. _____   9. _____   11. _____

7. _____   10. _____   12. _____

8. _____

13. When white light passes through a prism, it _____

    _____

    _____.

Directions The electromagnetic waves are listed in order by frequency in the electromagnetic spectrum. Write the names of the missing electromagnetic waves on the lines.

radio waves

14. _____

infrared rays
visible light
gamma rays

15. _____

ultraviolet rays

How Light Is Reflected

Directions What kind of mirror does each phrase describe?
Write *plane mirror*, *concave mirror*, or *convex mirror* on the line.

_____ **1.** flat, smooth surface

_____ **2.** surface curving outward at the middle

_____ **3.** image upside down and larger than real object

_____ **4.** causes light rays to come together in one focal point

_____ **5.** surface like the inside of a spoon

_____ **6.** surface of many rearview mirrors in cars

Directions Study each figure and answer the questions.

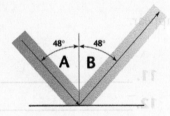

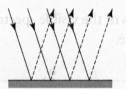
Smooth surface

Bumpy surface

7. Why are angles A and B equal in size?

_____

_____

_____

8. Which surface gives a clear image? Explain
your answer.

_____

_____

_____

Directions Answer each question.

9. Tell how reflected light waves and reflected sound waves are alike.

_____

_____

10. Tell how a mirror image and a hologram are different.

_____

_____

Sound and Light: Terms Review

Directions Match each term in Column A with its meaning in Column B.
Write the correct letter on the line.

Column A		Column B
_____ 1. photon	**A**	how high or low a sound is; determined by frequency
_____ 2. farsighted	**B**	the bending of light as it passes through a material
_____ 3. intensity	**C**	to bounce light or sound off a surface
_____ 4. plane mirror	**D**	form of energy that can be seen
_____ 5. pitch	**E**	able to see objects up close clearly
_____ 6. nearsighted	**F**	point where reflected light rays come together
_____ 7. refraction	**G**	a flat, smooth, clear reflecting surface
_____ 8. light	**H**	the strength of a sound, perceived as loudness or softness
_____ 9. reflect	**I**	tiny bundles of energy that make up light
_____ 10. focal point	**J**	able to see objects at a distance clearly

Directions Unscramble the word or words in parentheses to complete each sentence.

11. A(n) _____ is a sound wave reflected back to its source. (hoec)

12. A(n) _____ curves inward in the middle. (venocca rimror)

13. White light can be split into the _____. (blisive crumptes)

14. In order for sound to occur, matter must _____. (tearbiv)

15. The loudness or softness of a sound is its _____. (moveul)

16. One _____ measures one back and forth movement of a vibration. (leycc)

17. A(n) _____ helps correct nearsightedness. (navecoc snel)

18. A(n) _____ curves outward at the middle. (coxven roirmr)

19. A(n) _____ is produced by vibrations. (dunso evwa)

20. A human ear cannot hear a sound with a _____ of 10 Hz. (queencryf)

How Electricity Flows

Directions Write the correct word or words for each definition on the line. Then circle the word in the puzzle below.

1. a discharge of electricity from a cloud _____

2. a complete, unbroken path for electric current _____

3. an incomplete path for electric current _____

4. flow of electrons _____

5. Electricity is a form of _____. _____

6. kind of diagram that uses symbols to show parts of a circuit _____

7. unit that tells how much electric current flows through a wire _____

8. We measure electric _____ in amperes. _____

9. where an electric circuit begins _____

10. kind of electricity caused by a buildup of charge _____

P	B	C	C	S	D	V	I	V	U	K	R	O	U	B	E	E
T	H	P	D	A	E	S	F	D	S	T	A	T	I	C	L	L
N	A	Z	E	N	E	R	G	Y	J	I	A	U	O	Y	E	P
E	R	U	M	I	C	E	A	G	S	L	M	Z	A	Z	C	S
R	A	T	I	E	U	C	N	X	R	V	P	T	O	H	T	C
R	L	A	K	S	Q	I	P	L	F	M	E	I	T	K	R	H
U	L	Y	M	C	N	O	E	X	U	T	R	R	M	A	I	E
C	E	W	W	T	M	P	R	Y	T	N	E	V	F	H	C	M
E	L	E	H	R	P	T	E	O	I	S	K	U	S	P	I	A
P	C	G	V	E	O	P	E	N	C	I	R	C	U	I	T	T
C	I	N	R	U	R	D	N	J	G	H	E	P	N	O	Y	I
L	R	O	O	I	E	Q	T	O	O	C	B	R	N	T	F	C
J	C	L	O	S	E	D	C	I	R	C	U	I	T	H	S	O
A	F	C	P	D	X	I	O	N	S	P	N	T	S	G	P	T
R	Q	L	T	E	C	R	U	O	S	R	E	W	O	P	Y	N
C	N	T	O	R	L	D	H	W	Y	T	R	I	F	D	P	X

Conductors and Insulators

Directions Complete the outline by filling in the details about conductors and insulators.

Conductors and Insulators

A. Parts of an electrical cord

1. Wire: _____

2. Covering: _____

B. Some good electrical conductors

1. _____

2. _____

3. _____

4. _____

C. Some good electrical insulators

1. _____

2. _____

3. _____

4. _____

D. Resistance

1. Definition: _____

2. Unit used to measure it: _____

E. Three things the resistance of a wire depends on

1. _____

2. _____

3. _____

Some Sources of Electric Current

Directions Read the clues. Then complete the puzzle. Each term is related to sources of electric current.

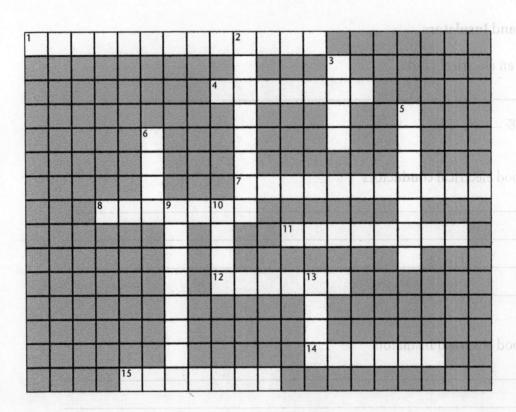

Across

1. kind of force that keeps current flowing in a circuit

4. kind of battery with a pastelike center (2 words)

7. kind of current that changes direction regularly

8. kind of battery with a liquid center (2 words)

11. kind of acid inside a battery

12. kind of current that flows in one direction

14. The current in our homes changes direction 60 times per _____.

15. energy that a power source gives to electrons in a circuit

Down

2. point where electrons leave or enter a battery cell

3. kind of sign that marks a positive terminal

5. source of voltage that changes chemical energy into electrical energy

6. metric unit that measures electromotive force

9. A battery changes _____ energy into electrical energy.

10. material that battery plates are made of

13. a wet-cell battery is found in most of these big machines

Using Ohm's Law

Directions Use Ohm's law to answer the following questions. The formula for Ohm's law is:

$$\text{current (amperes)} = \frac{\text{electromotive force (volts)}}{\text{resistance (ohms)}}$$

1. How much current does a headlight use with a 12-volt battery if it has a resistance of 3 ohms?

_____

2. How much current flows through a 100-ohm device connected to a 1.5-volt battery?

_____

3. What is the voltage of a 4-amp circuit with a resistance of 3 ohms?

_____

4. What is the resistance of a lightbulb that uses 0.5 amps and 110 volts?

_____

5. What is the resistance of an electric iron that takes 12 amps at 120 volts?

_____

6. What is the current used by a toaster with a resistance of 12 ohms if it uses 120 volts?

_____

7. What is the voltage of a 2-amp circuit with a resistance of 0.75 ohms?

_____

8. What is the voltage of a battery that produces a 1.5-amp current through a resistance of 8 ohms?

_____

9. What happens to the current in a circuit as the voltage increases?

_____

10. What happens to the current in a circuit as the resistance increases?

_____

Series Circuits

Directions Label the parts of the series circuit. Identify the *power source*, *wire*, *switch*, and *bulb* in the diagram of the series circuit. Draw arrows to show the direction of the electron flow.

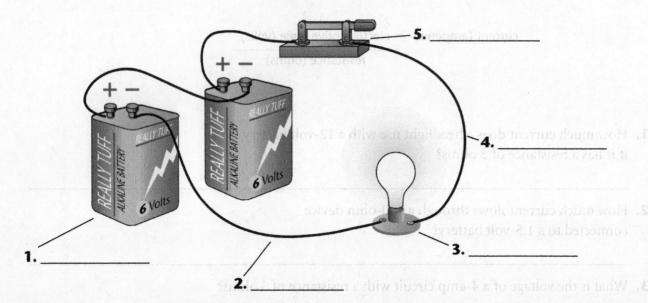

5. _____

4. _____

3. _____

1. _____

2. _____

Directions Choose an item from the box to complete each sentence.

add	disadvantage	fires	not work	series
circuit breaker	15	fuse	one	voltage

6. In a series circuit, electrons flow through _____ path.

7. One _____ of a series circuit is that all lights go out if one goes out.

8. If another electrical device were added to the circuit shown above, the _____ would be lower in each device.

9. To find the voltage of a series circuit, _____ the voltages of the cells.

10. If a series circuit had 3 batteries and each had 5 volts, the circuit would have a total of _____ volts.

11. The batteries of a flashlight often have a _____ circuit.

12. If one battery in a flashlight does not work, the flashlight will _____.

13. Fuses and circuit breakers prevent _____.

14. A _____ works by melting and breaking a circuit with hot wires.

15. A _____ switches off a circuit if it gets too hot.

Parallel Circuits

Directions The chart shows how a parallel circuit compares to a series circuit. Read the information, then complete the chart.

	Series Circuit	Parallel Circuit
1. Number of paths it has	one	
2. Advantages	Batteries in a series deliver more energy in the same amount of time.	
3. Disadvantages	If one light goes out, they all go out.	
4. What happens when electrical devices are added to the circuit?	Voltage is lowered in each device.	
5. What is the total voltage of batteries in the circuit?	total voltages of all the cells	

Directions Tell how many paths are in this parallel circuit.

6. _____

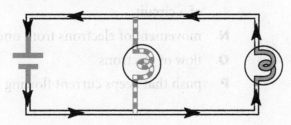

Directions Look at the 2 diagrams. Label one diagram *series circuit* and the other one *parallel circuit*. Then write the total voltage of each circuit.

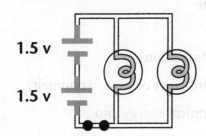

1.5 v
1.5 v

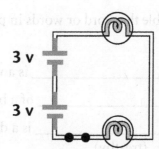

3 v
3 v

7. _____

9. Total voltage: _____

8. _____

10. Total voltage: _____

Electricity: Terms Review

Directions Match the terms in Column A with the meanings in Column B.
Write the letter of the answer on the line.

Column A

_____ 1. open circuit

_____ 2. dry-cell battery

_____ 3. direct current

_____ 4. series circuit

_____ 5. closed circuit

_____ 6. wet-cell battery

_____ 7. parallel circuit

_____ 8. circuit

_____ 9. alternating current

_____ 10. electric power

_____ 11. schematic diagram

_____ 12. electricity

_____ 13. Ohm's law

_____ 14. electromotive force

_____ 15. electric current

_____ 16. static electricity

Column B

A a type of circuit having more than one path for current

B a type of electricity that flows in only one direction

C electric power source with a liquid center

D an unbroken path for electric current

E rate at which electrical energy is used

F a type of circuit having only one path for current

G electric power source with a pastelike center

H a type of electricity that continuously changes direction

I an incomplete path for electric current

J a path for electric current

K current = voltage ÷ resistance

L buildup of electrical charge

M an illustration that uses symbols to show the parts of a circuit

N movement of electrons from one place to another

O flow of electrons

P push that keeps current flowing in an electric circuit

Directions Unscramble the word or words in parentheses to complete
each sentence.

17. A(n) _____ is a very poor conductor. (salurtion)

18. The _____ of a battery is where electrons enter or leave. (rainmelt)

19. A(n) _____ is a device that changes chemical energy into
electrical energy. (treatby)

20. Electricity passes easily through a(n) _____. (trunccodo)

What Are Magnets?

Directions Read the clues. Then complete the puzzle.

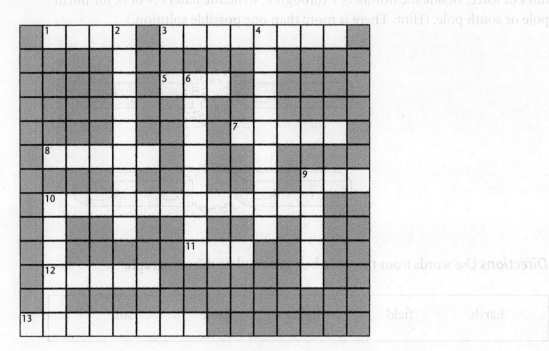

Across

1. Opposite poles of a magnet _____ together.
3. This magnet is shaped like something you can eat!
5. This animal sometimes swallows a magnet for its health.
7. Poles of the same type _____ each other.
8. the magnetic pole represented by the letter S
9. a machine that uses magnetism to view the human body
10. the end of a magnet (2 words)
11. A magnetic pole is located on each _____ of a bar magnet.
12. the magnetic pole represented by the letter N
13. The south pole of one magnet _____ the north pole of another.

Down

2. also known as *magnetite*
4. a magnet shaped like the letter U
6. _____ poles attract each other.
9. Magnets attract certain kinds of _____, such as iron.
10. it comes in several common shapes

Identifying a Magnetic Field

Directions Look at the two pairs of bar magnets. The broken lines represent their lines of force. Beside the numbers 1 through 8, write the letters *N* or *S*, for north pole or south pole. (Hint: There is more than one possible solution.)

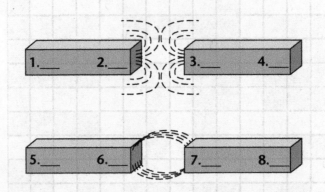

Directions Use words from the word box to complete the paragraph.

Earth	field	lights	pole	sun

9. _____ is like a giant magnet. It has a north and a south

magnetic **10.** _____. Like a magnet, the earth's magnetic

11. _____ is strongest at the poles. Electrically charged

particles from the **12.** _____ get trapped at the earth's poles.

They collide with molecules to create the spectacular northern **13.** _____.

Directions Write your answers to the questions on the lines.

14. Explain how you could use iron filings and a piece of paper to help reveal the effect of a magnetic field.

_____

_____

15. Why does the north pole of a compass point towards the earth's north magnetic pole?

_____

_____

Identifying Magnetism

Directions The figures represent magnetized and nonmagnetized material. Draw lines connecting the names of materials that *cannot* become magnets to Figure A. Draw lines connecting the names of materials that *can* be turned into magnets to Figure B. One is done for you.

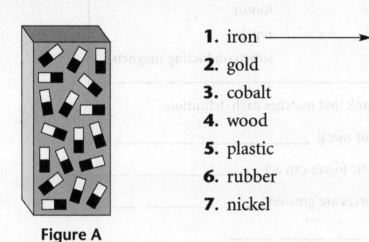

1. iron ⟶
2. gold
3. cobalt
4. wood
5. plastic
6. rubber
7. nickel

Figure A   **Figure B**

Directions Write your answers to the questions on the lines.

8. Are figures A and B realistic illustrations of materials? Explain your answer.

_____

_____

9. How did you know which figure showed a magnetized material?

_____

_____

Directions Write a word or words on each line to complete the story. You may use a word more than once.

As a science project, Miwako showed the class some of the properties of magnetism. First she

took a piece of **10.** _____ wire and stroked it several times with one end of a

11. _____. Then she demonstrated that the wire could pick up paper clips. It had

become a **12.** _____ with a north and a south **13.** _____.

Next she cut the wire in half with wire cutters. Guess what she ended up with?

14. _____ **15.** _____!

Magnets and Electromagnetism: Terms Review

Word Bank

alloy magnet	engine	magnetic field
attract	headphones	magnetic poles
core	lines of force	motor
electromagnet	maglev train	repel
electromagnetism	magnet	superconducting magnets

Directions Choose a term from the Word Bank that matches each definition.

1. an object that will attract certain types of metal _____

2. areas around a magnet in which magnetic forces can act _____

3. the end of a magnet, where magnetic forces are greatest _____

4. lines that show a magnetic field _____

5. the relationship between magnetism and electricity _____

6. a device that converts electrical energy to mechanical energy _____

7. to push apart _____

8. a temporary magnet made by passing an electric current through a wire wrapped around an iron core _____

9. to pull together _____

Directions There are six terms in the Word Bank that you did not use. Use them to complete the following sentences.

10. _____ can produce magnetic fields 200,000 stronger than Earth's.

11. In a home-made electromagnet, a nail can serve as the _____

12. A(n) _____ uses fuel such as gasoline to produce mechanical energy.

13. A(n) _____ is made of a mixture of metals.

14. A(n) _____ can travel at over 300 miles per hour.

15. _____ use electromagnets to change electric currents into sound waves.